SCREENPLAY

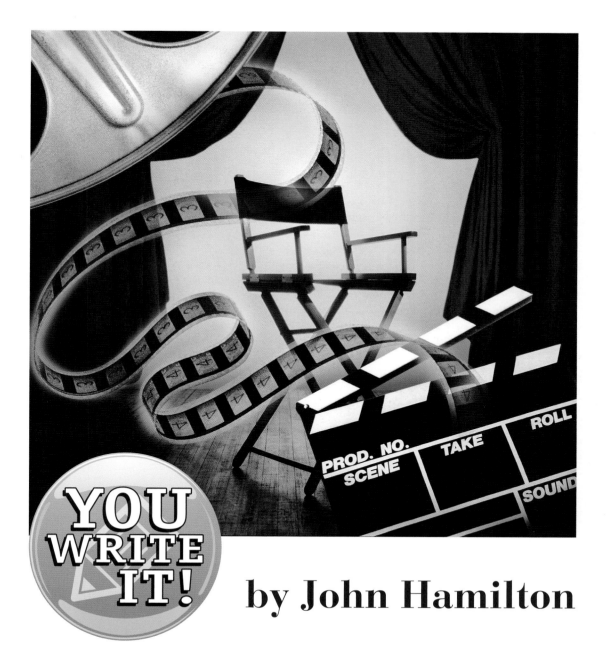

YOU WRITE IT!

by John Hamilton

VISIT US AT
WWW.ABDOPUBLISHING.COM

Published by ABDO Publishing Company, 8000 West 78th Street, Suite 310, Edina, Minnesota 55439.
Copyright ©2009 by Abdo Consulting Group, Inc. International copyrights reserved in all countries.
No part of this book may be reproduced in any form without written permission from the publisher.
ABDO & Daughters™ is a trademark and logo of ABDO Publishing Company.

Printed in the United States.

Editor: Sue Hamilton
Graphic Design: Sue Hamilton
Cover Design: Neil Klinepier
Cover Illustration: Spotlight
Interior Photos and Illustrations: p 1 Movie collage, Corbis; p 3 Film reel, Comstock; p 4 Film reel & tickets on silk, Comstock; Boy with clapboard, iStock; p 5 Girl at computer, iStock; p 6 Teen at computer, Comstock; p 7 Boy in library, Comstock; p 8 Director's chair, Comstock; p 9 *Heart of Osiris* Treatment, John Hamilton & Jim Ollhoff; p 10 Film lighting, iStock; p 11 *Fields of Gold* fly page, John Hamilton & Jim Ollhoff; p 12 *Fields of Gold* screenplay page, John Hamilton & Jim Ollhoff; *The Lighthouse*, John Hamilton; p 13 Screenwriter's software sample, courtesy Movie Magic Screenwriter; p 14 *The Complete Guide to Standard Script Formats*, courtesy CMC Publishing; p 15 Film and Clapboard, Comstock; p 16-17 *Fields of Gold* screenplay pages, John Hamilton & Jim Ollhoff; p 18 Indiana Jones, courtesy Paramount Pictures; p 19 Index card, iStock; pp 20-25 *The Wizard of Oz*, courtesy Metro-Goldwyn-Mayer; p 22 Comedy/tragedy masks, Comstock; p 26 Film reel, Comstock; p 27 Writers Guild of America West logo, courtesy Writers Guild of America West; p 28 William Goldman, AP Images; *Adventures in the Screen Trade: A Personal View of Hollywood and Screenwriting*, courtesy Warner Books; p 29 Michael Crichton, AP Images; *Jurassic Park III* still, Corbis; J. Michael Straczynski, AP Images; and p 32 Clapboard, Comstock.

Library of Congress Cataloging-in-Publication Data

Hamilton, John, 1959-
  You write it : screenplay / John Hamilton.
      p. cm. -- (You write it!)
  Includes bibliographical references and index.
  ISBN 978-1-60453-509-9
  1. Motion picture authorship--Juvenile literature. I. Title.

PN1996.H284 2009
808.2'3--dc22
                                2008044271

Contents

Introduction

"Grab 'em by the throat and never let 'em go."
—Billy Wilder

 A screenplay is like a blueprint. It is a master plan for constructing a film or TV show. It is also the key to a fantasy world, the world of Hollywood and movie stars. Who doesn't secretly dream of seeing their name in giant letters on the silver screen, for all the world to see?

Not everyone has Hollywood connections, or the ability to go from film school right to directing blockbusters. But almost anyone can write a screenplay. No matter who you are, no matter how humble your beginnings, an exciting screenplay with unforgettable characters might be your ticket to fame.

Of course, it's not really that simple. Thousands of people write screenplays each year, but only a tiny fraction of those stories ever get made into movies. You've got to know how to get your screenplay into the hands of the right people, and they have to accomplish the monumental task of actually getting the movie made. And even if the movie is produced, it might die at the box office. Still, writing screenplays is one of the most appealing, and possibly best-paying, careers that a writer can hope for. Perhaps *you've* got a screenplay you're dying to write. But where to start?

Novelist Gene Fowler once said, "Writing is easy. All you do is stare at a blank sheet of paper until drops of blood form on your forehead." What he meant is that writing is much harder than it looks. Anybody who can form a simple sentence thinks they can write. But *good* writing, like any other skill, takes practice.

Few people are born writers. However, there are certain skills anyone can learn. These "tools of the trade" can help you master the *craft* of writing. And once you've mastered the craft, you're well on your way to writing screenplays that others will love. You will encounter many obstacles along the way, but good writers find a way. The important thing is persistence, and a burning desire to tell your story.

Left: Do you have a screenplay idea that you want to write? Good writing, like any other skill, takes practice.

Ideas

"I steal from every movie ever made."

—Quentin Tarantino

The number one question asked of screenwriters is, where do you get your ideas? It's usually asked by insecure beginners who are afraid they don't have the imagination it takes to be successful. But as you'll soon find out, ideas are everywhere: in your head, in a book, in a movie, even in stray conversations overheard at lunch. Developing an idea into a *story* is where the hard work takes place.

How do you know if you have a good idea for a screenplay? Movies are great for showing action and motion, and for featuring sound. That is why action/adventure and special-effects-laden science fiction stories are so popular in today's theaters. It is difficult for movies to show stories that are *internal*—emotions or thoughts that happen only inside the minds of the characters. For example, your story might be about a young man who reads a self-help book and decides that he is a good person. That kind of story—where people think and feel about issues—is better left to novels and short fiction. In a film or video, the audience can only ever know what is seen and heard. Nowhere is the writer's motto "show, don't tell" more important than in a screenplay.

Characters in screenplays don't "think" or "realize" things. There must be visual cues that let the audience know what is happening, and it has to happen in the present tense. The best way to show emotion in a screenplay is to have characters taking action somehow. If two characters are having a heated argument, you can't write "Bill is angry with Tom." Instead, show Bill throwing a glass across the room, or leaving and slamming the door behind him. Use the medium to its full extent, and show emotions through cinematic action.

Coming Up With Ideas

- You must *read* in order to write. Read a lot. Every day. To see how screenplays are written, get your hands on the many scripts that are available both online and through various mail-order businesses. Your local library might also have scripts available for you to check out.
- Write what you know. Use your past experiences, then translate them into ideas.
- Brainstorm. Time yourself for two minutes. Jot down any ideas that pop into your head. Don't edit yourself, even if you think the ideas are stupid. They may spark even more creativity later.
- Keep a daily journal. It can be like a diary or a blog, but it can also include ideas that pop into your head, drawings, articles, photos, etc. As you collect information, you'll see patterns begin to emerge of things that interest you the most. Explore these themes.
- Write down your dreams. And your daydreams.

Organize Your Story

Most screenplays, especially Hollywood-type stories, follow a very tight structure. There are three acts representing a beginning, middle, and end. Within each act, the audience expects certain actions to take place, and certain characters to be introduced. Many student or independent films veer away from the traditional three acts, but it's a rare commercial film that succeeds without following this tried-and-true structure.

To help organize a script, many screenwriters use two tools: a beat sheet and a treatment. A beat sheet is simply a list of bullet points that briefly describe the major action taking place in the story. Depending on the level of detail you want to include, beat sheets can range from a single page to more than a dozen. Some writers use notecards instead of sheets of paper. Each notecard represents a scene. The cards can easily be shuffled around if you need to make room for more scenes.

A treatment is a longer kind of organizational tool. It is simple prose written in present tense, with very little dialogue, detailing all the major characters and plot elements of the screenplay. It can be a few pages long, or much longer, depending on how much detail you want to include. Some Hollywood screenwriters are hired to write scripts based on treatments that they have created.

For someone with no industry contacts, however, it's always best to actually complete a full script before trying to sell it. Treatments from beginners are rarely read or considered by producers, who prefer to read full scripts.

Think of a treatment as a very detailed road map that you can use when you're finally ready to write your script. Since it's for your own use only, you can write it in any format you prefer.

The Heart of Osiris
Treatment
by John Hamilton and Jim Ollhoff

Synopsis
A detective investigates a museum burglary and discovers a sect of Egyptian Osiris worshippers intent on delivering their god's long-lost heart to his mummy, thereby resurrecting him. To save his daughter's and girlfriend's souls, and the entire world, the detective must journey to the Egyptian underworld to defeat Osiris.

ATTEMPTED BURGLARY AT THE METROPOLITAN MUSEUM OF ART IN NEW YORK

A full moon rises over the imposing rooftop of the Metropolitan Museum of Art in the heart of Manhattan. The streets are nearly empty. It is very late.

The inside of the museum appears deserted. A light shines in a room way down the hall. As we enter the room, we see it is the Egyptian exhibit. Shadows play on the dusty antiquities.

A security guard turns from the window from which he has been watching the moon. He is counting money and sweating. He looks troubled.

A man stands on the other side of a security gate separating this room from the rest of the museum. He is powerfully built, and dressed in black. He broods as he waits impatiently.

The guard unlocks the gate and steps back. The mysterious stranger steps quickly into the room.

The man strides directly to a particular exhibit, which is labeled, "The Heart of Osiris." The exhibit is an ancient Horus jar with the head of a jackal. It is sealed shut, and covered with a glass exhibit case.

The man takes out what looks like a Geiger counter and tests the heart. The machine crackles alarmingly. Next he takes out what looks like herbs, places them in a small bowl near the jar. He takes out an amulet and begins to chant.

DETECTIVE CALHOUN GETS THE CALL

A telephone rings in the dark. We hear a grunt, a crash, and then a desk lamp flicking on. Detective Martin Calhoun has fallen asleep at his desk. When he turns on the light, he looks puzzled. A blanket is around his shoulders. On the desk are case files; photos of bodies, hair samples, witness statements. A newspaper clipping with a screaming headline: "Ripper strikes again." Calhoun's been doing his homework.

The phone rings incessantly. He reaches over to pick it up, spills coffee on his desk. "Hello," he says gruffly. Calhoun is a big man, with a slight paunch, but enough beef still on his bones to knock over a freight train. He's been around the block too many times; his temple is graying, and crow's feet crinkle around his eyes when he smiles, which hasn't been too often lately.

Screenplay Format

In Hollywood, a screenplay's purpose is to give guidance to the filmmakers and actors. It is only a guide. On the set, actors will interpret the lines you write for them in many ways. They will probably also make up lines of their own. The director will also create his or her own interpretation of your movie. Because of this, you do not have to write down every angle, camera move, or lighting setup. In fact, too many camera directions (such as CLOSE UP or CUT TO) may irritate the reader. Of course, if you are writing a script that you intend to direct yourself, then go ahead and include special camera, lighting, and sound directions. But if you are sending in your script hoping to have a Hollywood agent or producer purchase it, leave camera angles to the director—that's his or her job.

Script pages are designed so that one page equals roughly one minute of screen time (also called run time). If you have a lot of dialogue, the run time will be shorter. If you have a lot of action, one page might equal several minutes. Usually, though, one page equals one minute.

An average Hollywood script is between 90 and 120 pages. Action scripts and comedies are usually on the short end, about 100 pages. Dramas, because they have a lot of dialogue, often run longer. As a beginner, you shouldn't write a script longer than 120 pages.

Use heavy, plain white or pastel card stock as a cover for both the front and back of your script. The very first page is called the fly page. It contains the title of your script, about a third or halfway down the page, centered, in caps and in quote marks. A few spaces under that is the author's name, also centered (but not in all caps). In the lower left of the fly page is your contact information, single-spaced and left justified.

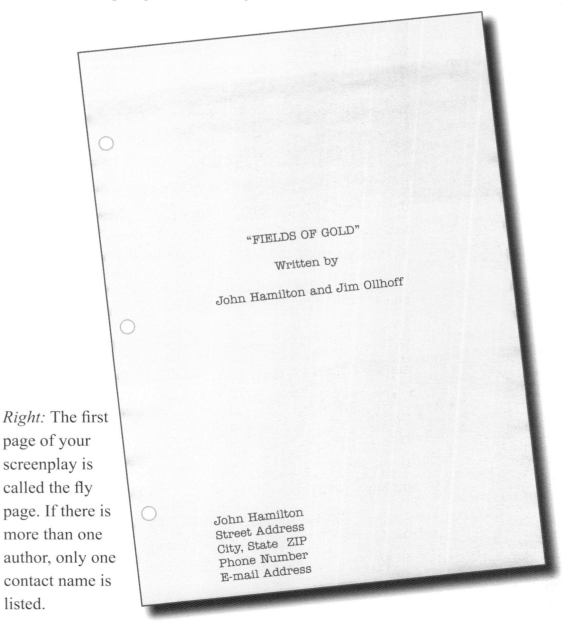

"FIELDS OF GOLD"

Written by

John Hamilton and Jim Ollhoff

John Hamilton
Street Address
City, State ZIP
Phone Number
E-mail Address

Right: The first page of your screenplay is called the fly page. If there is more than one author, only one contact name is listed.

Scripts should be printed on clean, white 8.5" x 11" paper, three-hole punched, printed on one side only. Do not include photos, illustrations, or diagrams of any kind. Type should be sized at 12 points, using some form of the Courier font (Courier New is fine). Even though people today write with computers and laser printers, scripts are still output to look like they were written on old manual typewriters. It's just something that's expected in the Hollywood culture.

Above:
Type your script using a Courier-like font.

Above: Although your pages are 3-hole punched, use only *two* brass fasteners on the top and bottom holes.

Here's another odd thing: even though your pages are three-hole punched, use only *two* brass fasteners, or brads, top and bottom, to bind the script together. If you use three brads, a snobby reader might think you're just a beginner, and won't give your script the respect it deserves.

In years past, scripts had CONTINUED written on the top and bottom of each page. That is no longer necessary. Also, do not number each scene. You might read scripts you buy in bookstores where each scene is numbered, but these are final "shooting" scripts used to produce the movie. Spec scripts (scripts that are written on "speculation" in the hope of having a producer buy it) do not have their scenes numbered, since the eventual director might want to rearrange or add elements.

Screenwriting Software

Most professional screenwriters use computer software that automatically puts text into screenplay format. This saves a lot of time in the writing process. Instead of worrying about the margin settings for each script element, like dialogue or scene descriptions, you can let the software do the work for you, allowing you to concentrate on your story.

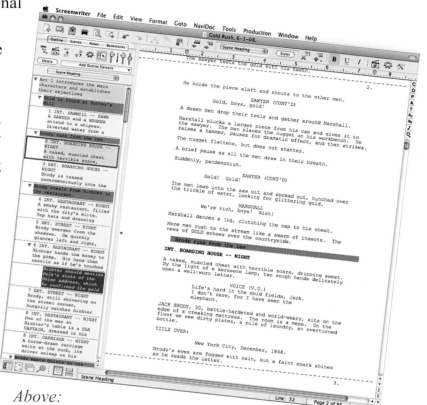

Above:

A sample of a script written using Movie Magic Screenwriter software. Another common screenwriting software program is Final Draft.

The two most popular screenwriting programs are Final Draft and Movie Magic Screenwriter, which can be found in stores or online retailers like Amazon.com. They do the job very well, but are expensive.

A cheaper alternative is to find add-ons to software you may already own. There are many free or low-cost templates to Microsoft Word available from several on-line retailers. Do a Google search for "Microsoft Word screenwriting software" to see what's currently available. There are also several free web-based screenwriting applications available, such as Zhura and Scripped.

The following page shows the kind of formatting that is generally accepted in a Hollywood feature film. There are too many special formatting considerations to include all of them in a book of this scope. Most questions can be answered with a simple Google search online (search term: screenplay formatting).

The definitive book about script formatting is by Hillis Cole and Judith Haag, called *The Complete Guide to Standard Script Formats*. It can be found in many libraries, or ordered from most bookstores or online book retailers. It also details the important differences between writing for feature films and television.

Don't worry *too* much about getting everything just right. If your script resembles the sample, then you should be okay. After all, the story is the most important thing.

Page Numbers

Starting on the second page of your script (not including the fly page), put the page number in the upper right corner of the script, followed by a period, about 0.5 inches (1.3 cm) down from the top edge of the paper. It is not necessary to include a running header with the script's title at the top of each page.

Left: Movies are written in a specific way. Details for how to correctly format your screenplay should be followed very carefully. It is especially important for first-time screenwriters to do this. By formatting your screenplay correctly, you are showing the reader that you know what you are doing.

Margins

There is no real "standard" setting for screenplay margins, but most professional scripts look a lot like the following examples. Screenplays have a top margin of about one inch (2.5 cm) to the body of the text. The bottom margin can be a little less or more because of rules for how each script element breaks from page to page. The left and right margins are different depending on the script element. Screenwriting software will handle these automatically for you, but if you are writing your script the old-fashioned way, use the tab settings on the following page.

Element	Left Margin	Right Margin	Width
Scene Heading	1.5″ (3.8 cm)	0.9″ (2.3 cm)	6.1″ (15.5 cm)
Action	1.5″ (3.8 cm)	0.9″ (2.3 cm)	6.1″ (15.5 cm)
Character Name	4.2″ (10.7 cm)	0.9″ (2.3 cm)	3.4″ (8.6 cm)
Dialogue	3.0″ (7.6 cm)	2.5″ (6.4 cm)	3.0″ (7.6 cm)
Parenthetical	3.7″ (9.4 cm)	2.9″ (7.4 cm)	1.9″ (4.8 cm)

❶ Scene Heading

Also called a slugline. Begin with an abbreviation "INT." or "EXT.", depending on whether the action takes place indoors or outside. Next comes the name of the location, all in capital letters. Next is a dash, and then the time of day, such as "NIGHT" or "DAY." Whenever the setting or time of day changes, write a new scene heading. Scene headings must not appear by themselves on the bottom of a page—they must appear together with an action.

❷ Action

Also called description. Keep it brief, sticking to story details. Don't tell the director where to place the camera. The first time a character is introduced, his or her name is written in all caps.

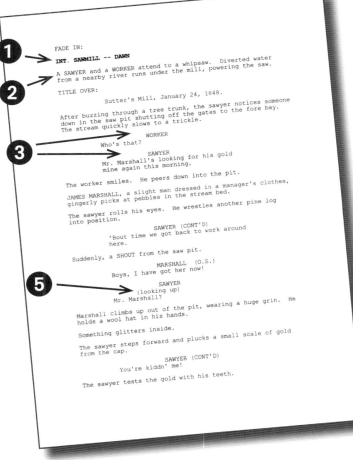

```
FADE IN:

INT. SAWMILL -- DAWN

A SAWYER and a WORKER attend to a whipsaw.  Diverted water
from a nearby river runs under the mill, powering the saw.

TITLE OVER:

        Sutter's Mill, January 24, 1848.

After buzzing through a tree trunk, the sawyer notices someone
down in the saw pit shutting off the gates to the fore bay.
The stream quickly slows to a trickle.
                        WORKER
        Who's that?
                        SAWYER
        Mr. Marshall's looking for his gold
        mine again this morning.

The worker smiles.  He peers down into the pit.

JAMES MARSHALL, a slight man dressed in a manager's clothes,
gingerly picks at pebbles in the stream bed.

The sawyer rolls his eyes.  He wrestles another pine log
into position.
                        SAWYER (CONT'D)
        'Bout time we got back to work around
        here.

Suddenly, a SHOUT from the saw pit.
                        MARSHALL  (O.S.)
        Boys, I have got her now!
                        SAWYER
                (looking up)
        Mr. Marshall?

Marshall climbs up out of the pit, wearing a huge grin.  He
holds a wool hat in his hands.

Something glitters inside.

The sawyer steps forward and plucks a small scale of gold
from the cap.
                        SAWYER (CONT'D)
        You're kiddn' me!

The sawyer tests the gold with his teeth.
```

❸ Character Name

Written in all caps. It is not necessary to use both a character's first and last name. If a character is heard but not seen, add V.O. (for "voice over") or O.S. (for "off screen") next to the name. Character names and their dialogue must never break between two pages. In other words, you can't have a character name on the bottom of one page, and his or her dialogue on the top of the following page.

❹ Dialogue

Sometimes dialogue is too long and must break between two pages. To handle this, type MORE (in parenthesis) below the dialogue at the bottom of the page. Then type CONT'D (in parenthesis) next to the character's name at the top of the following page. Hopefully, however, your dialogue is so crisp and direct that you won't have to resort to long paragraphs of spoken text.

He holds the piece aloft and shouts to the other men.   2.

                    SAWYER (CONT'D)
            Gold, boys, gold!   ◀── **❹**

A dozen men drop their tools and gather around Marshall. Marshall plucks a larger piece from his cap and gives it to the sawyer. The man places the nugget on his workbench. He raises a hammer, pauses for dramatic effect, and then strikes.

The nugget flattens, but does not shatter.

A brief pause as all the men draw in their breath.

Suddenly, pandemonium.

                    SAWYER (CONT'D)
            Gold! Gold!

The men leap into the saw pit and spread out, hunched over the trickle of water, looking for glittering gold.

                    MARSHALL
            We're rich, boys! Rich!

Marshall dances a jig, clutching the cap to his chest.

More men rush to the stream like a swarm of insects. The news of GOLD echoes over the countryside.

❶ ──▶

INT. BOARDING HOUSE -- NIGHT

A naked, muscled chest with terrible scars, dripping sweat. By the light of a kerosene lamp, two rough hands delicately open a well-worn letter.

                    VOICE (V.O.)   ◀── **❸**
            Life's hard in the gold fields, Jack.
            I don't care, for I have seen the
            elephant.

JACK BRODY, 30, battle-hardened and world-weary, sits on the edge of a creaking mattress. The room is a mess. On the floor we see dirty plates, a pile of laundry, an overturned bottle.

TITLE OVER:

            New York City, December, 1848.

Brody's eyes are fogged with pain, but a faint spark shines as he reads the letter.

❺ Parenthetical

These are short directions for the actor, placed between the character name and the dialogue. Used skillfully, they can take the place of unneeded action descriptions, which makes the reader's job easier.

Characters

"First, find out what your hero wants, then just follow him!"
—Ray Bradbury

What's more important, plot or character? Some writers say plot. After all, your readers are expecting a good story. On the other hand, think of the best movies you've ever seen. Chances are, what you remember most are the interesting characters.

The truth is, both elements are critical to good storytelling. You can't have one without the other. The reason characters are so memorable is because they are the key to unlocking the emotions of your story. You empathize with them, feel what they feel. Through great characters, you have an emotional stake in the outcome of the story. If you don't care about the characters, why should you care how the story turns out?

Character Biographies

Good writers are people watchers. Study the people you meet every day. Start a character journal; write down what makes these people interesting to you. Observe their physical characteristics and their behavior. What quirks do they have? How do they dress? How do they walk and talk? Mold and twist these traits into your own fictional characters.

Many writers find it helpful to create very detailed biographies of all their major characters. This sometimes helps you to discover your characters' strengths and weaknesses, which you can use later when you throw them into the boiling stew of your plot.

Backstory is the history you create for your characters. Most of it may never make it into your final draft, but it helps make your characters seem more "real" as you write.

Character Biography Checklist

Below is a list of traits you might want to answer for each of your characters. You should at least know this backstory information for your hero and main villain. What other traits can you think of that will round out your characters' biographies?

Character Biography Checklist
- ✓ Character's full name
- ✓ Nickname
- ✓ Age/Birthdate
- ✓ Color of eyes/hair
- ✓ Height/weight
- ✓ Ethnic background
- ✓ Physical imperfections
- ✓ Glasses/contacts
- ✓ Family background
- ✓ Spouse/children
- ✓ Religion
- ✓ Politics
- ✓ School
- ✓ Special skills
- ✓ Military
- ✓ Job/profession
- ✓ Hobbies/sports
- ✓ Bad habits
- ✓ Fears
- ✓ Hopes and dreams

The Hero

Above: Dorothy is the hero in *The Wizard of Oz.*

Your hero is your main character, or protagonist. He or she is the person the story is about. It's through the hero that your readers experience your story, and make an emotional connection with the other characters.

To make your hero likeable, make him or her a capable person. The hero should be competent enough to solve conflicts on her own, without calling in the cavalry. Give her a likeable trait or two. And be sure to give her a personal stake in the story. The audience will be much more engaged if the hero is personally threatened by the villain in some way.

Also, don't forget to give your heroes some flaws to overcome. This makes them seem more human, and interesting.

The Villain

Above: The Wicked Witch.

The villain is the antagonist of the story, the one who tries to keep your hero from accomplishing his or her goal. The most effective villains have weaknesses and motivations we can relate to. Nobody's afraid of a villain who's all bluster and anger.

An effective technique is to make your villain charming. It's what villains uses to lure their innocent victims. Charming villains are villains we love to hate.

Dialogue

Good dialogue propels the story. If you simply restate the obvious, then your dialogue is too "on the nose." After describing a fiery meteor hurtling through Earth's atmosphere, you probably don't need a character to point to the sky and say, "Look out! A meteor!" Instead, have him say something that also reveals his character. A hero might demonstrate his quick-thinking emergency skills by crying out, "Everyone to the bomb shelters! Children first!" In addition to giving information, good dialogue adds mood and suspense.

Secondary Characters

Secondary characters are critical in helping your hero overcome the problems you throw in his way. Some characters oppose the hero, which allows personality to be revealed through action and conflict.

Many types of secondary characters show up again and again in stories. Joseph Campbell, the great

Above: The Tin Man, Cowardly Lion, and Scarecrow are Dorothy's helpers on her journey through Oz.

scholar of mythology, identified many characters who have common purposes. He called them archetypes, a kind of common personality trait first identified by psychologist Carl Jung.

A *mentor*, or "wise old man or woman," gives critical help or knowledge to the hero. An obvious mentor character in *The Wizard of Oz* is Glinda the Good Witch, who gives Dorothy Gale the magical ruby slippers and instructs her to seek out the Wizard of Oz in Emerald City.

Threshold guardians, also called gatekeeper guardians, are characters who block the hero along the way. Threshold guardians can be thugs or minor villains your hero confronts. They test the hero, preparing her to battle the main villain later in the story.

Allies are helper characters who assist the hero. In *The Wizard of Oz,* the Scarecrow, the Tin Man, and the Cowardly Lion all help Dorothy in her journey through Oz. Note that at first, the Lion threatens Dorothy, acting as a threshold guardian. This is a good example of how two archetypes can combine in one character in the same story.

Plots

"Fiction is a lie, and good fiction is the truth inside the lie."

—Stephen King

Planning fiction, especially a long piece like a screenplay, can be a daunting task. It becomes more manageable if you break it down into smaller parts. You've probably already learned in school that fiction has three key elements: a beginning, middle, and an end. That seems simple enough. These are sometimes referred to as Acts I, II, and III. Acts I and III (the beginning and end) are critical pieces of the story, but are relatively short. Act II holds the guts of the story, where the majority of the action takes place.

The first 10 pages of a script are very important. Often called the "hook," this part of the story usually establishes the setting and major characters. Many writers, surprisingly, don't start their stories at the beginning. Instead, their scripts start with a bang, right in the middle of the action, with the hero embroiled in an exciting scene. Only after the scene's action is resolved do we take a step back and reveal the major characters and setting. Remember, character is action. By starting with an action scene, we automatically learn something about the main character.

After the beginning, how do you establish the plot and tie it all together? In *The Hero With a Thousand Faces*, author Joseph Campbell described patterns that are common to almost all works of fiction. They form a structure that authors use to tell the same basic tale, a story about a hero who goes on a quest to find a prize and bring it back to his or her tribe. This kind of story structure is very popular in Hollywood today.

Some writers think it's useful to keep this "hero's journey" in mind as they dream up their own stories. Of course, you don't have to rigidly follow the structure. It is merely a guide. But if you really study the movies made today, you'll discover many of the following elements hidden within.

Act I
The Ordinary World

This section introduces the hero before the adventure begins. Typical stories show the hero in his or her "normal" world, before a creeping evil upsets the balance of all things. Time spent in the ordinary world allows the writer to identify what the hero wants, and what's at stake.

The Call to Adventure

Also called an inciting incident, this is where an event happens that gets the story moving. There may be a message or temptation that calls your hero to act. The message is often delivered by a type of character, or archetype, called a herald, or a wise old man or woman.

Crossing the Threshold

This is the point where the hero makes a decision (or a decision is made for her), and she's thrown into the adventure. The hero's world is threatened, or changed, and it's up to the hero to make things right.

Act II

Tests and Conflict

Act II is for testing the hero. What allies does she meet? What enemies? Who is the chief villain, and what are her goals? Does our hero act alone, or does she gather a group together, a posse?

Act II is a series of rising actions and mini-climaxes. In real life, events happen in seemingly random order. But in a good story, each event the hero encounters is connected, leading to the next ordeal.

The Crisis

The crisis is a point in the story where the hero faces her most fearsome test yet, perhaps even enduring a brush with death. It's the "dragging the hero through the gutter" scene, where the hero's faith in herself is put to the ultimate test. Then the hero makes a realization, or figures out a puzzle, and sets off for the final conflict.

Act III

The Final Struggle

This is the point in the story where the hero uses everything he's learned and faces the ultimate test. In many films, the conflict becomes a physical action; the final struggle is a fight of some kind, using a combination of skills learned during the course of the story.

It's always best if your character wins the conflict on her own, especially if she uses skills learned during the course of the story. Beware of having another character swoop in to save the day. This kind of ending is called a *deus ex machina*, a Latin phrase that means "machine of the gods." In some ancient Greek plays, a cage with an actor portraying a god inside was lowered onto the stage, where he would miraculously solve the hero's seemingly hopeless problems. You've probably read books or watched movies where a similar event happened; an unexpected person or situation arises and saves the day. This is what some critics refer to as a contrived ending. Don't resort to this! You've spent the whole story building up your hero with new wisdom and skills. Let her save herself. Otherwise, what's the point of telling your story?

The Return

In many stories, the hero finally returns to her normal world. She brings back a prize, a symbolic magical elixir that benefits her people. Maybe it's gold, or medicine, or simply wisdom. But whatever the prize, what really matters is how the hero has changed (or didn't change) during her epic journey.

Get Produced

If you are making your own independent film, congratulations! You now have a screenplay you can use to create your own film or video. You've created an invaluable guide, a road map that will help make your dream of becoming a filmmaker a reality.

If you are a budding screenwriter who wants to break into Hollywood, you have a difficult task ahead of you. It's not impossible to sell a screenplay, but the competition is very, very steep. But if your story appeals to a wide audience, you might have a shot at seeing your script made into a Hollywood blockbuster.

Spec Script Writing

Most beginners write on "spec," or speculation. They complete a screenplay, without being paid, and then try to sell it to a producer. There is no "right" way to sell a screenplay. Maybe you have a friend of a friend who works in Hollywood and wants to read your script. Most beginners, however, don't know anybody in the business. Instead, they find an agent. Agents have film industry connections and sell scripts for their writer clients.

Getting an agent is hard, but not impossible. The usual steps include the following:

1. Register with the Writers Guild of America

The Writers Guild is a union of thousands of screenwriters. It helps make sure that screenwriters are treated fairly. Registering with the Writers Guild proves that your script is an original work, and discourages others from copying it or using it without your permission.

For details, go to their web site: http://www.wga.org/

2. Get a List of Agents

Lists of agents who consider new screenwriters are available at various web sites and in "writer's guide" books. You can also find free agency listings at the Writers Guild web site.

3. Send a Query Letter

Instead of sending your whole script, most agents want you to first send a short query letter that explains what your story is about.

4. Send Out Your Script

If interested, an agent will ask to see your completed script. Make sure you proof and spell-check it one last time, then send it along with a self-addressed stamped envelope (SASE). If the agent likes your script, he or she will offer to represent you and start shopping your work to the studios.

Final Thoughts

If your script is rejected, don't despair. Remember, the agent or producer isn't rejecting *you*, only your story. Maybe your writing is fine, but the studio isn't buying stories like yours at this time. Trends come and go in the marketplace, but don't try to write what you think studios are looking for. By the time you finish your screenplay, the fickle public will have moved on to the Next Big Thing. Simply write what you love, and the rest will follow.

You have the gift of storytelling. Sometimes you just need good timing and a little bit of luck. But remember, the more persistent you are, the luckier you'll get. Keep writing!

Screenwriter Profiles

"Writing is finally about one thing: going into a room alone and doing it. Putting words on paper that have never been there in quite that way before. And although you are physically by yourself, the haunting Demon never leaves you, that Demon being the knowledge of your own terrible limitations, your hopeless inadequacy, the impossibility of ever getting it right. No matter how diamond-bright your ideas are dancing in your brain, on paper they are earthbound."

William Goldman (1931-)

William Goldman is one of the most well-respected screenwriters in Hollywood. He won an Academy Award in 1969 for *Butch Cassidy and the Sundance Kid*, and in 1976 for *All the President's Men*. He has written dozens of screenplays and novels, including *Dreamcatcher*, *Last Action Hero*, *Misery*, *The Great Waldo Pepper*, and *The Princess Bride*. A popular reference book for budding screenwriters is Goldman's *Adventures in the Screen Trade: A Personal View of Hollywood and Screenwriting*.

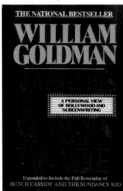

Above: A popular reference book.

"My dad was a journalist, so I saw him typing when I was growing up, so it seemed like a normal occupation, to sit down and type something as your job. I myself began writing pretty young. In the third grade we all had to do puppet shows and most of the kids just did a little skit. I wrote a nine-page play that my father had to type up for me, using carbon paper, so all the kids would know their parts. And I wrote a lot in fifth and sixth grade, too, and I became known for it; I was the weird kid who wrote extra assignments the teacher didn't ask for. I just did it because I liked writing so much. I was tall and gangly and awkward and I needed to escape, I guess." –Michael Crichton

(from michaelcrichton.com)

Michael Crichton (1942-2008)

Michael Crichton was a very popular writer of screenplays and novels. His science fiction and techno-thriller books have sold millions of copies worldwide. His screenwriting credits include *The Great Train Robbery* and *Twister*. He also co-wrote the film adaptation of his immensely popular dinosaur story, *Jurassic Park*.

"This is what newcomers need to hold onto. In the end, it doesn't matter what school you went to or who your contacts are. It comes down to the integrity of your storytelling… It's great to take the seminars and go to the parties, but you know what? Put your emphasis on little black marks on a piece of paper." –J. Michael Straczynski

(CreativeScreenwriting)

J. Michael Straczynski (1954-)

J. Michael Straczynski is an award-winning screenwriter and television producer. He was the producer and head writer of the popular science fiction television series *Babylon 5*, penning 92 episodes. He has since moved on to writing feature films, including the screenplay of director Clint Eastwood's *Changling*. He is also the author of a popular book for beginning writers, *The Complete Book of Scriptwriting*.

Helpful Reading

- *Making a Good Script Great* by Linda Segar
- *Screenplay: The Foundations of Screenwriting* by Sid Field
- *The Complete Book of Scriptwriting* by J. Michael Straczynski
- *The Writer's Guide to Writing Your Screenplay* by Cynthia Whitcomb
- *Adventures in the Screen Trade* by William Goldman
- *The Complete Guide to Standard Script Formats* by Judith H. Haag and Hillis R. Cole
- *The Writer's Journey: Mythic Structure for Writers* by Christopher Vogler
- *The Hero With a Thousand Faces* by Joseph Campbell
- *Stein on Writing* by Sol Stein
- *Self-Editing for Fiction Writers* by Renni Browne and Dave King
- *Writing Dialogue* by Tom Chiarella
- *Building Believable Characters* by Marc McCutcheon
- *Zen in the Art of Writing* by Ray Bradbury
- *The Elements of Style* by William Strunk, Jr., and E.B. White
- *The Transitive Vampire* by Karen Elizabeth Gordon
- *Roget's Super Thesaurus* by Marc McCutcheon
- *2009 Writer's Market* by Robert Brewer
- *Jeff Herman's Guide to Publishers, Editors, & Literary Agents 2009* by Jeff Herman

Glossary

Antagonist — Often called the villain, the antagonist is an important character who tries to keep the hero from accomplishing his or her goal.

Archetype — A type of character that often appears in stories. Archetypes have special functions that move the story along, such as providing the hero with needed equipment or knowledge.

Backstory — The background and history of a story's characters and setting. When writing, it is good to know as much backstory as possible, even if most of it never appears in the final manuscript.

Beat Sheet — An organizational tool used by screenwriters. Beat sheets are outlines that briefly describe the action that takes place in the story.

Fly Page — The very first page of your screenplay. It contains the title of the script, the author(s) name(s), and the author's contact information.

Hook — The beginning of a story, used to grab a reader's interest.

Parenthetical — Short directions for an actor placed between the character name and the dialogue in the script. A parenthetical, such as "looking up," can help take the place of unneeded action descriptions.

Protagonist — A story's hero or main character. The protagonist propels the story.

Screen Time — Actual minutes of a produced movie. Each page of a script is equal to roughly one minute of screen time. Screen time is also called "run time."

Slugline — Another name for a scene heading, such as INT. SCHOOL – DAY.

Spec Scripts — These are scripts that are written by an author "speculating," or guessing, that a producer will want to buy it. Most beginners write spec scripts.

Treatment — A long outline of a screenplay. Treatments are written in present tense, with little or no dialogue.

Index